IMPORTANT JOBS

ON MOVIE SETS

by Mari Bolte

PEBBLE

a capstone imprint

Published by Pebble Explore, an imprint of Capstone
1710 Roe Crest Drive, North Mankato, Minnesota 56003
capstonepub.com

Library of Congress Cataloging-in-Publication Data is available on the Library of Congress website.

ISBN 9780756572242 (hardcover)
ISBN 9780756572198 (paperback)
ISBN 9780756572204 (ebook PDF)

Summary: Gives readers basic info about often and less often-considered jobs on movie sets.

Image Credits
Alamy: Agencja Fotograficzna Caro, 6, Eamon O'Doherty, 17, Entertainment Pictures, 21, PictureLux/The Hollywood Archive, 9, ZUMA Press, Inc., 27; Getty Images: Geber86, 14, John Eder, 5; Newscom: Splash News, 18; Shutterstock: DC Studio, Cover (bottom), Frame Stock Footage, 22, Gorgev, 13, Gorodenkoff, 10, 25, guruXOX, 28, pui_bunny, Cover (top left), Sergey Novikov, Cover (top right)

Editorial Credits
Editor: Mandy R. Robbins; Designer: Dina Her; Media Researcher: Jo Miller; Production Specialist: Tori Abraham

All internet sites appearing in back matter were available and accurate when this book was sent to press.

Printed and bound in China.   PO5132

TABLE OF CONTENTS

Words in **bold** are in the glossary.

ON THE BIG SCREEN

Who doesn't love a good movie? The comedy, the action, the drama! Watch them in a theater. Press play at home. Or bring them anywhere with a phone. But they don't just make themselves!

Many people work together to make movies. Find out what they do. Every job is important!

ACTORS

Actors are the people you see on the screen. They bring characters to life. Sometimes they do action scenes. They train hard to get in shape.

Acting is more than reading lines off a page. Actors must work with other actors. They can show a character's thoughts or feelings. Being funny or good at singing or dancing are other ways to act. Actors can be any age, **gender**, race, or physical ability.

SPECIAL EFFECTS ARTISTS

Special effects artists make imaginary things seem real. Robots that run on wheels or spaceships that fly are special effects. Special effects artists make tiny **sets** that look like actual places.

Artists use computers too. They can make imaginary creatures. They can even make explosions! A good artist can make anything a movie might need.

> ### FACT
> Superhero movies are expensive to make. Each Marvel movie costs between $100 and $200 million. *Avengers: Endgame* cost $350 million!

DIRECTORS

Directors are in charge of the creative parts of a movie. Only they know what they want the movie to look like. They make sure the **script** makes sense. They choose actors. They help the actors understand the story.

The movie needs to stay on **budget** and on time. That is the director's job too. A good director is organized. They are also good at working with people.

PRODUCERS

Producers are the people who get movies made. Sometimes they come up with new ideas. Sometimes they read scripts and pick their favorites. They also find a way to pay for the movie.

If the director needs more money, the producers get it. If people do not agree, they find a solution. Good producers are problem solvers.

FACT

Sometimes, actors are also producers. They might want to work on new or different types of projects. Or they might just like to make movies.

WRITERS

A movie is only as good as its script. Most of your favorite lines are thanks to a writer. A writer can make a book into a movie. Or they might have a brand-new idea. Sometimes they turn a bad script into a good one.

Writers can work alone or together. It might take more than one writer to come up with a movie script.

SET DESIGNERS

Sets are where movies are filmed. A set might include a room or a building. Everything in that room is part of the set. A set designer makes sure the set looks like the real thing. They choose items that belong in that space. Every wall, piece of furniture, or decoration you see in a movie scene is planned by the set designer.

Sometimes, the cameras move. A set designer makes sure you never see anything that doesn't belong.

CRAFT SERVICES

Making movies can take months. It is hard work! People making the movie must eat. Leaving to get food wastes time. Craft services has food ready at all times. They set out tables.

Crew members can stop for a snack or a meal. If a movie is being shot in the desert, craft services supplies plenty of cold water to drink. They also clean up any messes.

ANIMAL TRAINERS

Some movies use animals. Actors might ride horses. They could have a pet. Dangerous animals add drama.

Trainers teach animals what to do. The animals learn where to stand. A dog will bark when the trainer tells it to. Some animals can do tricks. They carry items. They jump over things. Good movie animals behave while on set. When animals cooperate, making the movie is easier.

ANIMATORS

Animators draw creatures and bring them to life onscreen. Most use computers for this. They might create a made-up being. It needs to look real next to a person.

Other times, the whole movie must be drawn. This is the case with cartoon movies. Animators work with directors and designers. They try to make sure every detail is right.

Some movies are shot in front of a green screen. The actors pretend action is happening around them. But really, they are in a room painted green. Later, animators add in backgrounds and objects. The backgrounds cover everything green. It can look like actors are in another country or even on another planet.

Bright neon green is usually used. That's because few things are that color. Nothing the actor wears can match the green screen. It wouldn't show up!

COMPOSERS

A movie's story is important. But so is the music! Music helps you know when to feel happy or sad. It adds excitement. When something scary is about to happen, you will know.

A good **composer** writes music that matches what is happening on-screen. Did you leave the theater humming music from the movie? Then the composer was good!

FACT

John Williams is a famous movie composer. You have probably heard his music before! He has worked on series like Jurassic Park, Star Wars, and Harry Potter.

There are many people needed to make a movie. The things you see, hear, and feel are thanks to movie makers. Everyone needs to work together. If one part is not done well, the whole movie is not a success. Would you want to work on a movie set? What job would you do?